TABLE OF CONTEN

MW00568053

Encouraging Interest

Help students to develop an understanding and appreciation for character education themes through reading stories. A list of picture books is included in this teacher resource.

Black Line Masters and Graphic Organizers

Encourage students to use the black line masters and graphic organizers to present information, reinforce important concepts and to extend opportunities for learning. The graphic organizers will help students focus on important ideas, or make direct comparisons.

Character Cards

Use the character cards provided as a springboard for discussions, role-playing or to sort according to different character traits shown. The teacher may also wish to enlarge the cards while photocopying and use them as a base for a good character bulletin board display.

Role-Playing

Role-playing offers an excellent opportunity for students to become sensitive to how others feel in different situations and to develop empathy. Be sure to introduce role-playing only after class members become familiar and comfortable with each other. In addition, set rules for role-playing to prevent inappropriate behavior. In order for students to get the most out of role-playing, include:

- an enactment of the scenario presented
- a discussion and analysis of the scenario presented
- further role-playing of alternatives
- drawing conclusions regarding the scenario presented

SELF-ESTEEM / PRIDE

Self-Esteem: to demonstrate a positive opinion of yourself
Pride: delight or satisfaction in your accomplishments, achievements and status

Activity 1: Student of the Week

Student of the Week is not only a great way to promote self- esteem and to instill pride, but will encourage students to learn more about their classmates and to create a community. At the beginning of the school year, have families choose the week that their child will be Student of the Week. In preparation for that week ask families to send in special photos such as baby photos to display, and a bag of items that the student would like to share. Dedicate a bulletin board display with the student's information, pictures and school work. The teacher may also wish to include written notes from the other students that compliment or recognize the child chosen for student of the week.

Activity 2: Celebrating Students

Acknowledge and celebrate children's accomplishments and positive qualities on an ongoing basis using the various certificates provided in this teacher resource. Keep track of which certificates have been handed to whom in order to watch out for certain behaviors or accomplishments for certain students. Certificates can be given out in the moment, or the teacher may wish to hold a regular class meeting to recognize students.

Activity 3: Perseverance

Have students set personal goals. Encourage students to persevere and to achieve their goals by:

- Affirm to students your confidence that they can achieve their goals
- Give students honest feedback on what students are doing well and what they need to work on
- If a task seems overwhelming to a student, break it down into smaller more manageable parts
- Let students know that it is "ok" if something is not easy, and they can work through obstacles
- Stress the importance of "finishing what you have started"
- Talk about your own experiences
- Celebrate accomplishments and have students express how they feel when achieving their goal

Activity 4: Developing Good Work Habits

Help students take responsibility for their learning. Encourage students to self–assess their daily work habits using kid friendly and easy to understand criteria. The How Am I Doing? rubric provided in this teacher resource will clarify what makes a good piece of work exemplary and the qualities of an excellent student.

___________________________'S GOAL

My goal is to ___________________________

I want to achieve this goal because

____

To achieve this goal I need to

____

STUDENT OF THE WEEK

Student Of The Week: ______________________________

Dear Parent/Guardian,

Your child has been chosen to be *Student of the Week* for the week of ____________________.
Please fill in the paper bag with special items from home that your child would like to bring back to share with our class. Be sure to include photos of your child's choice to display on our *Star of the Week* bulletin board display. In addition, please complete the information below to add to the d isplay.

Your family's participation and support is greatly apprectiated!

My favourite book:

____

My favourite food:

____

The best thing I like about school is:

____

STUDENT OF THE WEEK

My name is ____

This is a picture of me.

I am ____________ years old. I am special because ____________________________

____

______________________________'s

BOOK OF PRIDE

I am proud
when
I learn
something
new at
school.

I am proud of my work.

I am proud when I win at something.

I am proud
when
I can do
something
well.

Draw a picture.

I am proud of me!

SHARING OUR PRIDE

Complete the sentence inside the balloon.

I CAN DO IT!

by:

____

I am going
to learn
to read!
I can do it!

I am going
to learn
to play
the trumpet!
I can do it!

I am going
to practice
to be the
best soccer
player
I can be!
I can do it!

I am going
to save
up my
money for
something
special!
I can do it!

I am going
to practice
to be the
best dancer
I can be!
I can do it!

I am going
to learn
to play
basketball!
I can do it!

I am going
to keep
trying until
I can do it!

COMPASSION

To be sympathetic and understanding toward the needs and feelings of others

Activity 1: People Have Feelings

Generate a class list of different kind of feelings. Discuss situations that might occur around each feeling. Have students complete the My Feelings worksheets and discuss.

Activity 2: Caring People

Ask students, "What does it mean to be a caring person"? As a whole group brainstorm a list of do's and don'ts for being caring. Ask for specific examples of each behavior they identify.

Discussion Starters:

1. How do you think a new student feels when coming to a new class? What could you do?
2. What could you do to make a sad person happy?

Activity 3: Acts Of Kindness

Brainstorm with students what it means to be kind. Record their responses on chart paper. Next go through the student generated list and have students associate the kind of feelings they have around each act of kindness. Encourage students to understand that they have the ability to make someone happy, perhaps by complimenting them or doing something kind. Have students make compliment or appreciation cards for students in the class or create coupons to give out to people as an act of kindness.

Discussion Starters:

1. How does it feel to be kind? How does it feel to be mean?

Activity 4: When People Feel Angry...

Ask students to remember a time when they felt angry. Have students explain what happened and how they handled the situation. Some situations might include:

- something is unfair
- someone was mean or teased us
- something was broken
- someone is in our space
- someone is not sharing
- something has been taken away from us.

Activity 5: Bullying

Help students gain a clear understanding of bullying. Bullying can be described as the act of hurting someone physically or psychologically. Students should also be made aware that bullies come in all shapes and sizes. Usually someone is bullied repeatedly. Some forms of bullying include:

Physical: hitting, punching, tripping, shoving, stealing belongings, locking someone in or out etc.
Verbal: teasing, putdowns, taunting, or making embarrassing remarks etc.
Relational: excluding someone from a group, spreading rumours, or ignoring someone

It is the hope that if students can understand what a person feels like when bullied, students will develop empathy and help stop bullying.

MY FEELINGS

1. 	I feel happy when...
2. 	I feel sad when...
3. 	I feel worried when...

MY FEELINGS

4. 	I feel excited when...
5. 	I feel angry when...
6. 	I feel scared when...

HOW WOULD YOU FEEL?

Describe how you would feel in each situation.

Situation	I would feel...
I am going to visit my favourite cousins.	
My pet fish died.	
I am moving to another school.	
It's my birthday.	
I had a test.	
Someone bullied me at school.	
My friend told me a funny joke.	
I had to try something for the first time.	
A special event got cancelled.	

ACTS OF KINDNESS

Acts of kindness let people know that you care about them.
Colour the boxes that are examples of acts of kindness.

listening

sharing your snack

being bossy

using manners

cooperating with others

including someone in a group

being helpful

being rude

teasing someone

COURTESY

Polite, considerate behavior toward others.

Activity 1: Courtesy

Ask students if they know what the word courtesy or polite means. As a class, brainstorm a list of courtesy do's and don'ts. Create a class big book based on the list generated by the students.

Discussion Starters:

1. Why is it important to be polite to other people?
2. How do you feel when someone is polite to you?
3. How do you feel when you are polite?
4. How do you think others feel when you are polite to them?
5. Can you think of examples of how you can be polite to others today?

Activity 2: Encouraging Respect

Ask students what does it mean to treat other people with respect? Generate a class list of do's and don'ts for treating people with respect in different situations such as when there is a class visitor. Post the list up on a wall as a reminder for students. Some of the do's and don'ts may include: be courteous and polite, listen to others without interrupting, treat other people the way you want to be treated, don't give people put downs or treat them badly, and don't judge people before you get to know them.

Activity 3: People Are Alike

Encourage students to think about how people can be alike, but still unique. Survey students on a variety of topics and create whole class graphs to demonstrate how people can be similar and/or different. Some survey ideas include: birthday months, favourite colours, number of people in their household and favourite foods. In addition, celebrate the differences that students have.

Discussion Starters:

1. What do they notice?
2. What surprised them?

Activity 4: Friendship

Ask students to define friendship and if they think they have to be a good friend to have a good friend. Create a class "recipe" of behaviors for being a good friend. Discuss each one and have students name classmates who demonstrate each behavior. Some behaviors might be someone who: shares, is helpful, is kind, is fair, is fun or is a good sport.

Discussion Starters:

1. I think the friendship behavior I am best at is…
2. I think the friendship behavior I need to work on is…

_______________________'s

BOOK ABOUT COURTESY

I show courtesy when I wait for my turn to speak.

I show courtesy when I use a tissue.

I show courtesy when I don't interrupt someone.

I show courtesy when I say, "thank you"!

I show courtesy when I use good table manners.

I APPRECIATE YOU!

Thank you for...

______________________________'s

BOOK ABOUT BEING A FRIEND

Being a friend means sharing.

Being a friend means taking turns.

Being a friend means helping each other.

Being a friend means having fun.

This is a picture of my friend and me!

MY FRIEND

Name ____

What is a friend?

____

____

Name a friend from school. ______________________

Draw a picture of something you like to do together.

Write about your picture.

____

____

____

____

ALL ABOUT FRIENDS

Name ____

Who is your best friend?

Draw a picture of something you like to do together.

Write about your picture.

Why is this person your best friend?

ALL ABOUT FRIENDS

Pretend there is a new student in class. What would you do to make friends with the student and make them feel welcome?

Draw a picture of something you can do together.

GETTING ALONG

Colour the picture.

What does this picture show?

RESPONSIBILITY

To carry out a duty or task carefully and thoroughly; be able to count on, depend or trust

Activity 1: Families Work Together

As a whole group, ask students if they think families are important and to explain their thinking with examples. Then ask children to think about special contributions each family member makes to the family. Record the student responses on a chart. Put checkmarks or tally marks to show repeat answers. Encourage students to think about their own role in their family. What do they contribute? How is it helpful to the family? Give students a family chart to take home and record how their family works together.

Activity 2: Rules and Responsibilities at Home

As a whole group, brainstorm different rules that students have at home. List the different rules on a chart and poll the students if they have each rule at their home. Some of the rules that might be stated are: I have a bedtime, I am not allowed to go near the stove without an adult, I need to be polite, I need to tidy up my toys, etc.

Discussion Starters:

1. Which rules keep you safe at home?
2. Which rules help keep you healthy?
3. Which rules help the members of your family to get along?
4. What do you think would happen if you didn't have any rules at home?
5. What rules would you change? Why?

Activity 3: Rules and Responsibilities at School

Using paper strips, have the students brainstorm classroom or school rules together. Some rules might include: Walk in the hallways, keep your hands to yourself, be polite, ask permission to go to the bathroom etc.

Discussion Starters:

1. Ask the students which rule they feel is the most important.
2. Who do you think should make up the rules in the classroom or at school? Explain your thinking.
3. Which rules help keep you safe?
4. Which rules help you learn?
5. What are your responsibilities at school?
6. What are the responsibilities of the people who work at your school?
5. Are there different rules for inside the school and outside the school?

Activity 4: Rules in Public Places

Do the same as above, but while talking about public places.

FAMILY MEMBERS WORK TOGETHER

Name ____

Please fill out this chart to help your child develop an understanding of how families function and how various family members contribute. For example sister, - helps feed the baby. Parents - cook meals. Encourage your child to think about their own role in your family. What do they contribute? How do they help?

Family Member	Job or Contribution

RESPONSIBILITIES AT HOME

Colour the pictures that show a child taking on responsibility at home.

RULES ARE IMPORTANT

A rule at ____

____

This rule is important, because

____

____

____

_______________________'s

BOOK ABOUT RESPONSIBILITY

I am responsible at home when I help to vaccum.

I am responsible at home when I help dry the dishes.

I am responsible at home when I help fold clothes.

I am
responsible
for me
when I tie
my own
shoes.

I am
responsible
for me
when I
brush my
teeth.

I am responsible at school when I do my work.

I am responsible at school when I follow the rules.

FAIRNESS

Being truthful and just.

Activity 1: What is Fairness?

Discussion Starters:

1. What does treating people fairly mean?
2. Have you ever said, "That's unfair"?
   How do you know when something is unfair?
3. Have you ever played a game when someone cheated? How did you feel about it?
4. Does fairness mean enforcing the same rules for everyone, even if it means losing a game?

Activity 2: Honesty is the Best Policy

As a whole group ask students what they think the expression, "honesty is the best policy" means. Do they agree with the expression? Have students explain their thinking.

Discussion Starters:

1. Would you trust somebody who lies? Who cheats? Who steals? Why, or why not?
2. Have you ever told the truth, even though that was a difficult thing to do? Explain.

Activity 3: Making Good Decisions

Encourage children to learn to think about whether something is right or wrong before making a choice of how they will proceed in different situations. Role play the different scenarios found on the good character cards in this book. Compare and discuss what happens in each scenario with children who choose to do the "right thing" and with children who choose to do the "wrong thing". How would children feel after each decision? What are the consequences?

Discussion Starters:

1. What can you think about before deciding if doing something is right or wrong?
3. What do you think would happen if nobody cared about doing the "right thing"?
4. Do you agree with "finder's keepers, loser's weepers"? Explain your thinking.

Activity 4: What is Conflict Resolution?

Introduce the idea of conflict resolution to students. Conflict resolution is a process to help solve problems in a positive way. Each person involved is encouraged to take responsibility for their actions. For younger children the teacher may wish to refer to it as, "working it out". Clear steps for conflict resolution might include:

- What is the problem?
- Listen without interrupting.
- Talk it out.
- Come up with different solutions.

Discuss and review the above process with students. Role-play different situations so students can practice walking through the process. Students should be encouraged to try to understand the other person's perspective of a conflict. The teacher may wish to use situation that are reflected to their class. Encourage students to come up with different solutions so they get in the habit that if a solution does not work, to try to find another one. In addition, post the steps for conflict resolution on the board for easy student reference.

DISCUSSION STARTER CARDS

GOOD CHARACTER DISCUSSION STARTER

One of your classmates needs a red crayon, but doesn't have one. You have a red crayon.

What could you do?

GOOD CHARACTER DISCUSSION STARTER

You see someone on the schoolyard who fell and is crying.

What would you do?

GOOD CHARACTER DISCUSSION STARTER

Name a fair way to decide who goes first in a game.

Explain your reasons.

GOOD CHARACTER DISCUSSION STARTER

You are lining up for lunch and see someone's money fall out of their pocket.

What is the right thing to do?

GOOD CHARACTER DISCUSSION STARTER

You are really upset that someone has taken your favourite pencil off your desk.

What would you do?

GOOD CHARACTER DISCUSSION STARTER

Who is someone you admire?

Explain your reasons.

DISCUSSION STARTER CARDS

GOOD CHARACTER DISCUSSION STARTER

There is a new student in your class. What would you do to make them feel welcome?

GOOD CHARACTER DISCUSSION STARTER

There is a special toy you would like to buy and you don't have enough money right now.

What can you do?

GOOD CHARACTER DISCUSSION STARTER

You want to get your caregiver's attention, but they are on the phone.

What should you do?

GOOD CHARACTER DISCUSSION STARTER

Your mother wants you to get ready for bedtime, but you don't want to.

What should you do?

GOOD CHARACTER DISCUSSION STARTER

You have just spilled something at home and have made a big mess.

What should you do?

GOOD CHARACTER DISCUSSION STARTER

How can you show that you use your time wisely at school?

Explain your reasons.

_______________________'s

BOOK ABOUT FAIRNESS

I show
I am fair
by taking
turns.

I show I am fair by playing by the rules.

I show I am fair by treating people the way I want to be treated.

I show I am
fair because
I think
about how
my actions
will affect
others.

I show
I am fair
because
I don't
blame
others for
my mistakes.

CONFLICT SCENARIO CARDS

CONFLICT SCENARIO CARD

The teacher has told you to line up for recess. Someone in the class pushes their way in front of you instead of going to the end of the line.

What would you do?

CONFLICT SCENARIO CARD

Someone in the class has taken your materials without your permission.

What would you do?

CONFLICT SCENARIO CARD

You are building a structure using construction materials and someone comes and knocks it down on purpose.

What would you do?

CONFLICT SCENARIO CARD

You and your friends are playing with a ball at recess. Another kid comes along and takes the ball away.

What would you do?

CONFLICT SCENARIO CARD

You and your and best friend get into an argument.
Your best friend does not want to play with you anymore.

What would you do?

CONFLICT SCENARIO CARD

You are trying to do your work at your desk and the same person keeps bothering you.

What would you do?

WORK IT OUT!

What is the problem?

Listen without interrupting.

Talk it out.

Come up with different solutions.

CITIZENSHIP

Being law abiding and involved in service to school, community and country.

Activity 1: What is Citizenship?

Introduce the idea of citizenship to students in a whole group setting. Reinforce with the children that they all have something to contribute to the class, school and community.

Brainstorm a list of useful things that children could do to help out in class, at home, in the school and within the community.

Discussion Starters:

1. Ask students how they feel after they have helped someone.
2. Ask students how they feel after they have been helped.
3. Identify people who they know that volunteer at school or in the community and talk about why they do it.
4. How does obeying the rules show that you are a good citizen?
5. How do community workers make the community a better place?

Activity 2: Making a Difference

As a whole group brainstorm a list of people who may be of need. Encourage students to think about people they know, or situations such as children in impoverished countries. In addition, discuss charities that children might be familiar with and any fundraising activities they have participated in at school or with their families.

Give the students in your class the opportunity to practice citizenship by taking part in a school or community project. Some ideas include:

- Planting a school garden
- Collecting toys for needy children
- Collecting clothes for a shelter
- Participating in a book drive for the school or shelter
- Collecting school supplies for children in impoverished countries
- Collecting loonies for a charity
- Participating in a trash pick-up day
- Going on a class field trip to a senior citizens' home to perform songs or to sit and play games with the residents

Activity 3: Citizenship Class Collage

Create a class citizenship collage using words, artwork, and pictures cut out from magazines or newspapers.

OUR COMMUNITY WORKERS

What kind of community worker would you want to be?

Draw a picture.

How does this community worker help the community?

CITIZENSHIP CREST

Design a citizenship crest to let people know how to be a good citizen.

________________'s

BOOK ABOUT CITIZENSHIP

I am a good citizen because I try to make the world a better place.

I am a
good citizen
because
I care
about the
environment.

I am a
good citizen
because
I follow
the rules.

I am a
good citizen
because
I take
part in the
community.

I am a
good citizen
because
I treat
people with
respect.

BRAIN STRETCH

What I think know...

What I wonder about..

CHARACTER CARDS

CHARACTER CARDS

CHARACTER CARDS

CHARACTER CARDS

CHARACTER CARDS

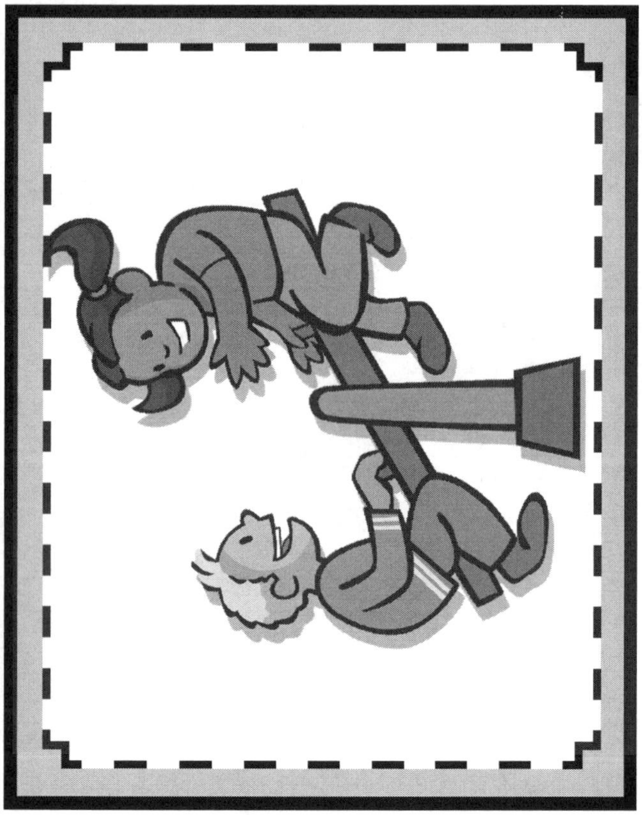

responsibility

courtesy

citizenship

friendship

compassion

fairness

THINKING ABOUT GOOD CHARACTER

My Journal about:

_________________________'s

GOOD CHARACTER DIARY

Ideas for your diary:

- Write about the ways you have been a good citizen.
- Write about ways you have shown courtesy.
- What have you done to achieve a special goal?
- How have you shown you are responsible?
- How have you shown you are good friend?

GOOD CHARACTER DIARY

Monday

GOOD CHARACTER DIARY

Tuesday

GOOD CHARACTER DIARY

Wednesday

GOOD CHARACTER DIARY

Thursday

GOOD CHARACTER DIARY

Friday

GOOD CHARACTER DIARY

Saturday

GOOD CHARACTER DIARY

Sunday

GOOD CHARACTER SONG

To The Tune Of, "*If You Are Happy And You Know It, Clap Your Hands*"

If you are "character trait"
and you know it, clap your hands!

If you are "character trait"
and you know it, clap your hands!

If you are "character trait"
and you know it, and you really want to show it.... .

(have a child give an example of how to demonstrate the character trait)

If you are "character trait"
and you know it, clap your hands!

A WEB ABOUT...

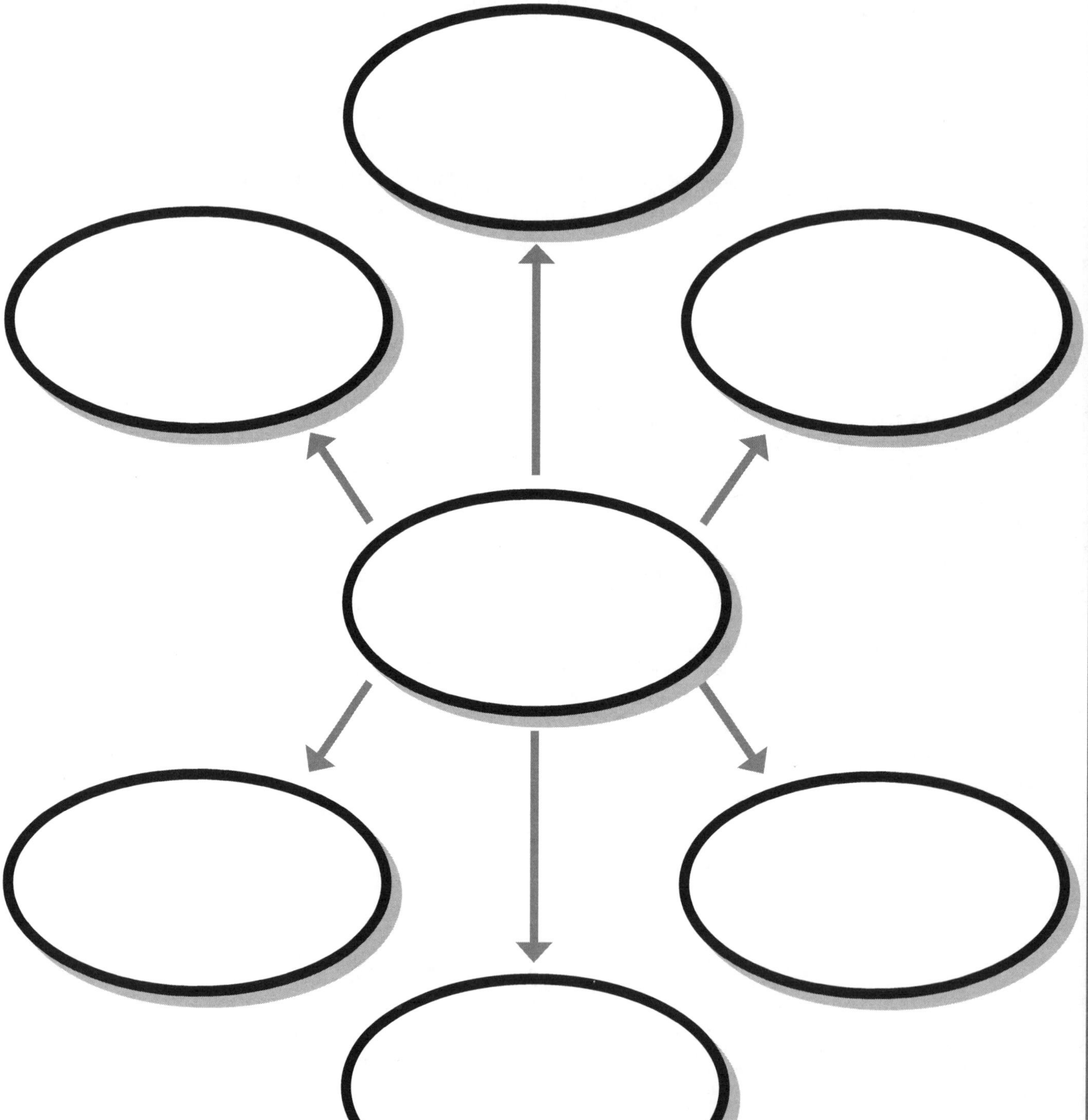

T-SHIRT TIPS

Design a t-shirt that gives tips on how to be______________________________

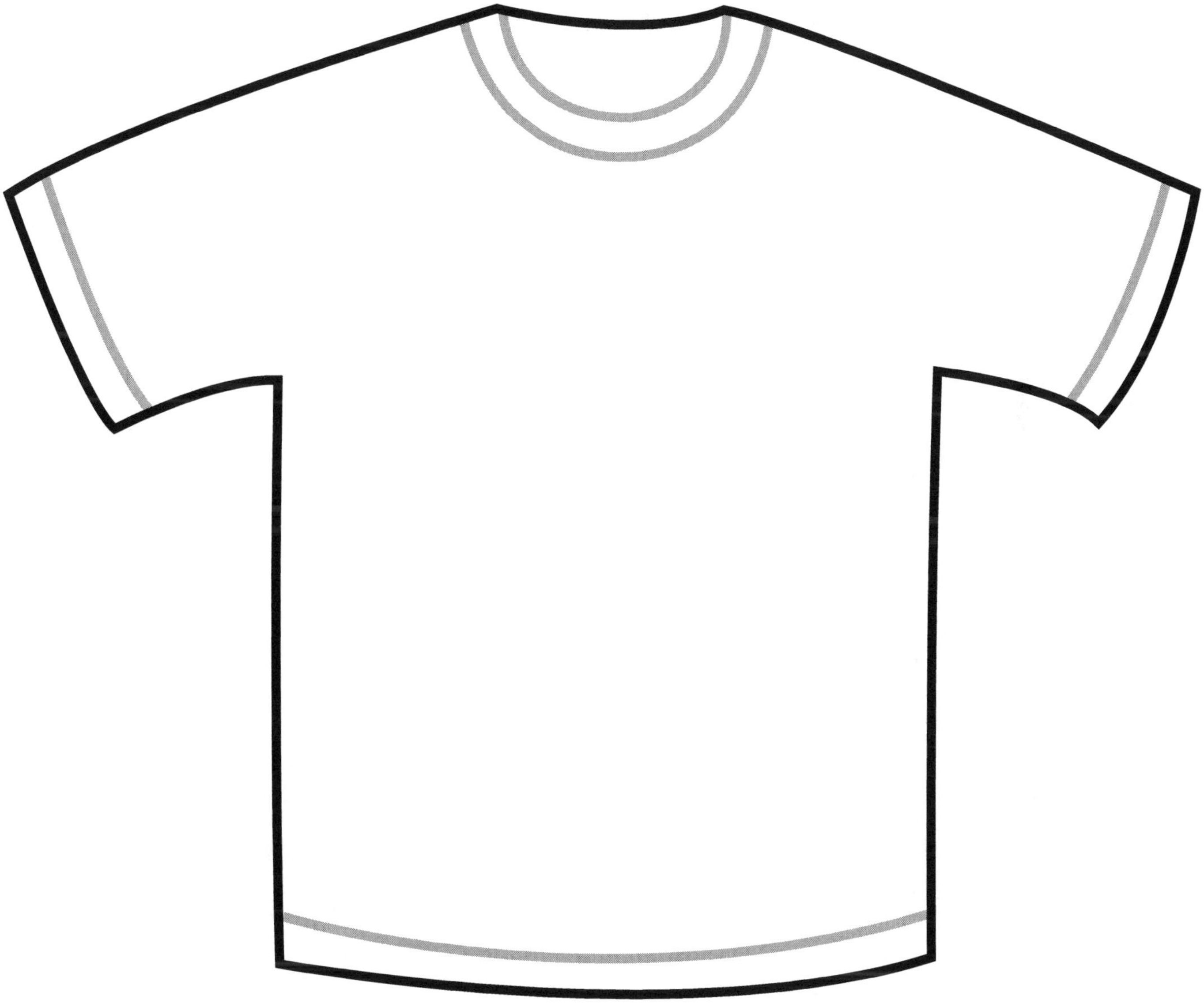

A T-CHART ABOUT...

CREATE A STAMP

Write about your stamp.

RESPONSIBILITY AWARD

Keep up the effort!

GREAT FRIEND AWARD

This award is for:

____

COURTESY AWARD

KEEP UP THE EFFORT!

TOP MANNERS!

THIS AWARD IS FOR:

____

GREAT JOB!

Keep up the effort!

SUPER SPORTSMANSHIP!

This award is for:

____

CITIZENSHIP AWARD

KEEP UP
THE EFFORT!

Community Helper AWARD

This award is for

____

STUDENT PARTICIPATION RUBRIC

LEVEL	STUDENT PARTICIPATION DESCRIPTOR
Level 4	Student consistently contributes to class discussions and activities by offering ideas and asking questions.
Level 3	Student usually contributes to class discussions and activities by offering ideas and asking questions.
Level 2	Student sometimes contributes to class discussions and activities by offering ideas and asking questions.
Level 1	Student rarely contributes to class discussions and activities by offering ideas and asking questions.

UNDERSTANDING OF CONCEPTS RUBRIC

LEVEL	UNDERSTANDING OF CONCEPTS DESCRIPTOR
Level 4	Student shows a thorough understanding of all or almost all concepts and consistently gives appropriate and complete explanations independently. No teacher support is needed.
Level 3	Student shows a good understanding of most concepts and usually gives complete or nearly complete explanations. Infrequent teacher support is needed.
Level 2	Student shows a satisfactory understanding of most concepts and sometimes gives appropriate, but incomplete explanations. Teacher support is sometimes needed.
Level 1	Student shows little of understanding of concepts and rarely gives complete explanations. Intensive teacher support is needed.

COMMUNICATION OF CONCEPTS RUBRIC

LEVEL	COMMUNICATION OF CONCEPTS DESCRIPTOR
Level 4	Student consistently communicates with clarity and precision in written and oral work. Student consistently uses appropriate terminology and vocabulary.
Level 3	Student usually communicates with clarity and precision in written and oral work. Student usually uses appropriate terminology and vocabulary.
Level 2	Student sometimes communicates with clarity and precision in written and oral work. Student sometimes uses appropriate terminology and vocabulary.
Level 1	Student rarely communicates with clarity and precision in written and oral work. Student rarely uses appropriate terminology and vocabulary.

CHARACTER EDUCATION PICTURE BOOK LIST

ANTI-BULLYING

"Oliver Button is a Sissy", written by Tomie dePaola
"Benny Gets a Bully Ache", written by Jane Bomberge
"Big Bad Bruce", written by Bill Peet
"Martha Walks the Dog", written by Susan Meddaugh

COMPASSION

"Berenstain Bears and the In-Crowd", written by Jan & Stan Berenstain
"Frog and Toad Are Friends", written by Lobel, Arnold
"A Chair For My Mother", written by Vera B. Williams

FRIENDSHIP

"Alexander and the Windup Mouse", written by Leo Lionni
"Best Friends", written by Steven Kellogg

HONESTY / FAIRNESS

"It's Not Fair!", written by Charlotte Zolotow
"The Berenstain Bears And the Truth" written by Jan & Stan Berenstain
"Alexander And The Terrible, Horrible No Good, Very Bad Day", written byJudith Viorst

MANNERS

"Manners", written by Aliki
"What Do You Do Dear", written by Seysle Joslin

PERSERVERANCE

"A Weed Is A Flower", written by Aliki
"Green Eggs and Ham", written by Dr. Seuss
"Mike Mulligan and His Steam Shovel", written by Virginia Lee Burton
"The Very Busy Spider", written by Eric Carle
"The Little Engine That Could", written by Watty Piper

PRIDE

"The Summer of the Swans", written by Betsy Byars
"Captain Tom Cat", written by Bill Martin Jr
"The Trumpet of the Swan", written by E. B. White

RESPECT

"Goldilocks and the Three Bears", written by various authors
"Grandfather Counts", written by Andrea Cheng

RESPONSIBILITY

"Berlioz the Bear", written by Jan Brett
"Now One Foot, Now the Other", written by Tomie dePaola
"Horton Hatches the Egg", written by Dr. Seuss
"Strega Nona: An Old Tale", written by Tomie dePaola

HOW AM I DOING?

	COMPLETING MY WORK	USING MY TIME WISELY	FOLLOWING DIRECTIONS	KEEPING ORGANIZED
 FULL SPEED AHEAD!	• My work is consistently complete and done with care • I added extra details to my work	• I consistently get my work done on time	• I consistently follow directions	• My materials are consistently neatly organized • I am consistently prepared and ready to learn
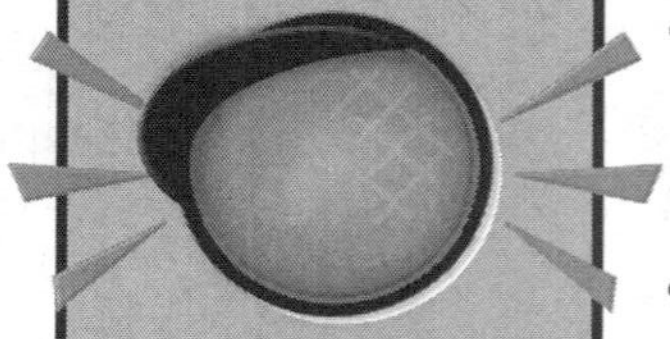 KEEP GOING!	• My work is complete and done with care • I checked over my work	• I usually get my work done on time	• I usually follow directions without reminders	• I usually can find my materials • I am usually prepared and ready to learn
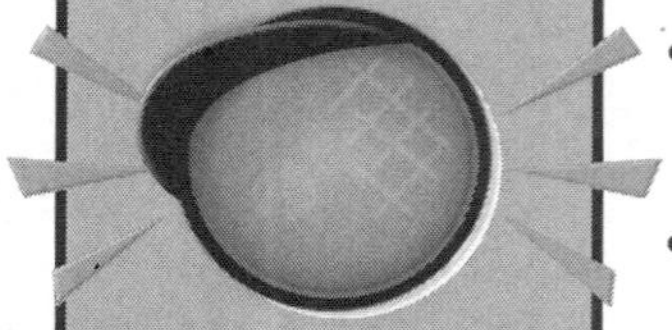 SLOW DOWN!	• My work is complete • I need to check over my work	• I sometimes get my work done on time	• I sometimes need reminders to follow directions	• I sometimes need time to find my materials • I am sometimes prepared and ready to learn
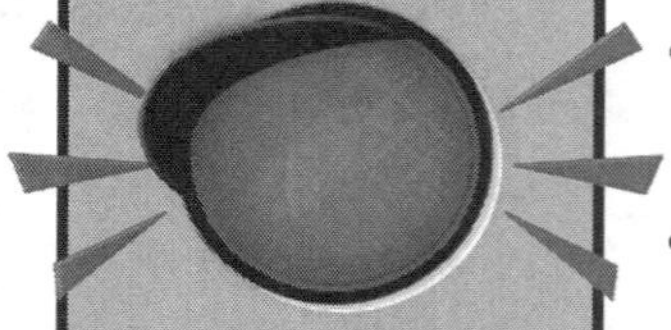 STOP!	• My work is not complete • I need to check over my work	• I rarely get my work done on time	• I need reminders to follow directions	• I need to organize my materials • I am rarely repared and ready to learn